First-Generation Immigrant Families

THE CHANGING FACE OF MODERN FAMILIES

First-Generation
Immigrant Families

Julianna Fields

Mason Crest Publishers, Inc.

MASON CREST PUBLISHERS INC.
370 Reed Road
Broomall, Pennsylvania 19008
(866)MCP-BOOK (toll free)
www.masoncrest.com

First Printing

9 8 7 6 5 4 3 2 1

ISBN 978-1-4222-1499-2
ISBN 978-1-4222-1490-9 (series)
Library of Congress Cataloging-in-Publication Data
Fields, Julianna.

Produced by Harding House Publishing Service, Inc. www.hardinghousepages.com
Interior Design by MK Bassett-Harvey.
Cover design by Asya Blue www.asyablue.com.
Printed in The United States of America.

Although the families whose stories are told in this book are made up of real people, in some cases their names have been changed to protect their privacy.

Photo Credits

Creative Commons Attribution ShareAlike: Nancy Coop 37, Karpov the Wrecked Train, Liuzzo, David 33, saeru 38, swanksalot 54; Dreamstime: Zenpix 48; United States Army: Hyde, Sgt. 1st Class Gordon 47, United States National Guard: Greenhill, Sgt Jim 51

ontents

Introduction

The Gallup Poll has become synonymous with accurate statistics on what people really think, how they live, and what they do. Founded in 1935 by statistician Dr. George Gallup, the Gallup Organization continues to provide the world with unbiased research on who we really are.

From recent Gallup Polls, we can learn a great deal about the modern family. For example, a June 2007 Gallup Poll reported that Americans, on average, believe the ideal number of children for a family to have these days is 2.5. This includes 56 percent of Americans who think it is best to have a small family of one, two, or no children, and 34 percent who think it is ideal to have a larger family of three or more children; nine percent have no opinion. Another recent Gallup Poll found that when Americans were asked, "Do you think homosexual couples should or should not have the legal right to adopt a child," 49 percent of Americans said they should, and 48 percent said they shouldn't; 43 percent supported the legalization of gay marriage, while 57 percent did not. Yet another poll found that 34 percent of Americans feel a conflict between the demands of their professional life and their family life; 39 percent still believe that one parent should ideally stay home with the children while the other works.

Keep in mind that Gallup Polls do not tell us what is right or wrong. They don't report on what people should think—only on what they do think. And what is clear from Gallup Polls is that while the shape of families is changing in our modern world, the concept of family is still vital to our sense of who we are and how we interact with others. An indication of this is the 2008 Gallup poll that found that three out of four Americans reported that family values are important, while one in three said they are "extremely" important.

And how do Americans define "family values"? According to the same poll, here's what Americans say is their definition of a family: a strong unit where faith and morals, education and integrity play important roles within the structure of a committed relationship.

The books in the series demonstrate that strong family units come in all shapes and sizes. Those differences, however, do not change the faith, integrity, and commitment of the families who tell their stories within these books.

1 Coming to America

Terms to Understand

global: relating to the whole world.

endanger: to expose to risk or threat.

infant mortality: the rates of deaths among children in their first year of life.

work ethic: a set of values that include the importance of hard work and its effect on a good character.

mainstream: relating to the most prominent and well accepted groups, styles, beliefs, etc.

discrimination: when a person is treated differently because of some category to which that person belongs, rather than being judged as an individual.

racism: the belief that race is a factor in judging the abilities, characteristics, or worth of a person.

Azuka, Aurelio, Alesky, and Mai are in the same seventh-grade home-room. They live in the same city, and they share many things in common. All four are first-generation immigrants. Azuka's parents are from Nigeria; Aurelio's are from Guatemala; Alesky's were born in Poland; and Mai's are from Vietnam. The four young people are all Americans, but in some ways, their families are different from other American families.

As the twenty-first century progresses, however, families like these will become more and more common. The United States has always been a nation of immigrants, but as our world becomes increasingly *global*, immigrants are coming from all parts of the globe. In nearly every state in the country, the number of immigrant families is growing.

This trend scares some people. Some Americans worry that if too many immigrants come to the United States, our country will no longer be the same nation that it used to be. They are frightened that immigrants may *endanger* America's values; that they may cost American taxpayers too much money; and that they may take away jobs from Americans who were born in this country. People who have these concerns are often in favor of putting tighter restrictions on America's immigration policies.

But whatever laws might be passed in the future, there is no way to turn back the clock. Immigrant families are here now, and they and their children will help shape America's future. Luckily, these families bring many strengths with them to this country.

Strengths of Immigrant Families

Researchers have found that on average, first-generation immigrant children are healthier than those born to U.S.-born mothers. *Infant mortality* rates are lower among immigrant families, and their babies are less likely to be born with low birth weights. (Low birth weight often indicates other more serious health concerns throughout a child's life.) The children of immigrants have fewer

Terms to Understand

prejudice: opinions or ideas about a person, group, or thing, formed before knowing much about him, her, or it.

disillusioned: having lost faith and trust in one's beliefs, ideals, etc.

pessimistic: having a tendency to stress the negative; believing that the worst is most likely.

controversial: characterized by strong opinions both for and against, and capable of stirring up conflict and debate.

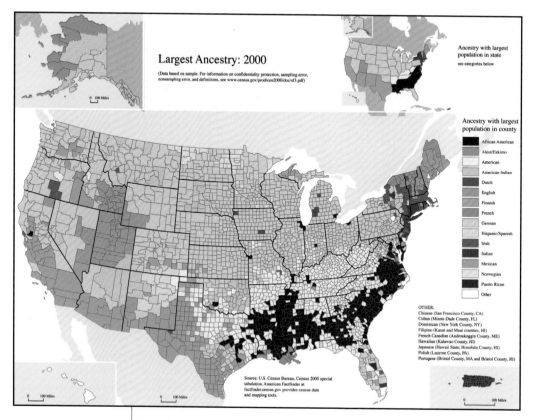

Largest Ancestry: 2000

(Data based on sample. For information on confidentiality protection, sampling error, nonsampling error, and definitions, see www.census.gov/prod/cen2000/doc/sf3.pdf)

Ancestry with largest population in state
see categories below

Ancestry with largest population in county

- African American
- Aleut/Eskimo
- American
- American Indian
- Dutch
- English
- Finnish
- French
- German
- Hispanic/Spanish
- Irish
- Italian
- Mexican
- Norwegian
- Puerto Rican
- Other

OTHER:
Chinese (San Francisco County, CA)
Cuban (Miami-Dade County, FL)
Dominican (New York County, NY)
Filipino (Kauai and Maui counties, HI)
French Canadian (Androscoggin County, ME)
Hawaiian (Kalawao County, HI)
Japanese (Hawaii State; Honolulu County, HI)
Polish (Luzerne County, PA)
Portugese (Bristol County, MA and Bristol County, RI)

Source: U.S. Census Bureau, Census 2000 special tabulation. American Factfinder at factfinder.census.gov provides census data and mapping tools.

Immigrants to the United States come from all over the world. This map shows the breakdown of populations in different parts of the country.

DID YOU KNOW?
According to the 2000 Census, 1 of every 5 children in the United States is a child of immigrants—that is, either a child who is an immigrant or who has at least one immigrant parent.

injuries and diseases, and they are less likely to have asthma.

Emotionally, children in immigrant families also often do better than those of U.S.-born families. This may have to do with the fact that most immigrant children live with both their biological parents, unlike many U.S.-

born families. They are also more likely to live within a large extended family that provides additional support to the entire family.

Immigrant families have a strong sense of pride and **work ethic**. Parents are willing to work hard, and they expect their children to do the same. As a result, the children of immigrants tend to have high educational goals, and they are less likely than children of U.S.-born families to engage in risky behaviors such as substance

When immigrant families arrive in America, they often settle in communities with others from their same country of origin. Fellow immigrants in these communities can help a family adjust more quickly to their new home by showing them where to shop, where to go to school, and where to go worship. They can also explain American society's various systems and traditions, which might otherwise be mysterious and overwhelming for new immigrants. These strong communities can also be supportive of the child's emotional and academic adjustment by reinforcing cultural values and parental authority, and by buffering them from *mainstream* society's pressure. The community may make the difference in a young person's life, helping her to maintain positive goals despite the challenges she faces as a newcomer to this country.

Among all children with U.S.-born parents, 12% have mothers and 12% have fathers who are not high school graduates. Among children with foreign-born parents, however, 23% have mothers and 40% have fathers who are not high school graduates.

abuse, early sexual intercourse, and delinquent or violent activity. Studies have shown that they also tend to spend more time doing homework and that they do better in school, at least through middle school. Even though their reading test scores are somewhat lower (because they often speak English as a second language), eighth-grade children of immigrants have slightly higher

This political cartoon, drawn in 1880, illustrates the concept that the United States is a safe refuge, welcoming all immigrants who seek a better life than they had in their home countries.

grades and math test scores than young adults of the same ethnicity in U.S.-born families.

These strengths, along with a strong sense of community, can help protect children of immigrants from some of American society's negative influences—but they are not always enough to help these young people overcome all the challenges they face.

Challenges Faced by Children of Immigrants

The children in immigrant families often have limited language skills with which to cope with a new country—and their parents are equally at a loss, which means their parents are not in a position to help them navigate some of adolescence's many challenges.

Children in immigrant families are far more likely than children in U.S.-born families to have parents who have not graduated from high school. As a result, the parents may be less able to help their children with homework, as well as unable to help them handle school in ways that will make the children more successful.

Because immigrants are likely to have less education, as well as poor English skills, many immigrant parents find themselves working in lower-paying jobs. They are often among workers who are paid the least and have the fewest benefits (such as health insurance).

Language is another challenge that first-generation immigrants face. Speaking two languages can be a

The percentage of children of immigrant families living in a single-parent household is only about 16%, compared with 26% for children of U.S.-born families. And nearly 40% of immigrant children live with other relatives and non-relatives in their homes, compared with about 22% for children of U.S.-born families.

Among all children in this country, 18% speak a language other than English at home. Among children in immigrant families, 72% speak a language other than English at home.

strength—but if no one in household is able to speak English fluently, the family will have problems finding work, talking with teachers and other school personnel, and dealing with doctors and social services.

Some of the greatest challenges children of immigrants face are *discrimination* and *racism*. *Prejudice* can set apart children of immigrants from mainstream populations, which may mean they have fewer resources and encounter lower teacher expectations. From the perspective of these students, school may become the focal point for discrimination, and they may perceive that they have no chance of success. Children from immigrant backgrounds typically enter school with very

Immigration is a *controversial* topic in the United States today. The answers to these questions are important to many Americans:

- How many immigrants should we continue to admit?
- Should future immigration be restricted to specific nations and/or races?
- On what should we base these policy decisions?
- How should we enforce these policy decisions?

What do *you* think?

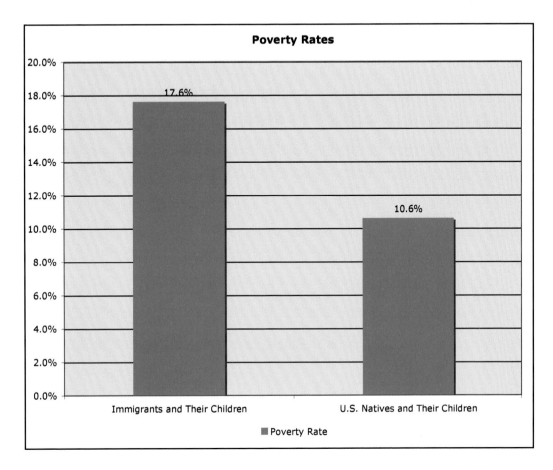

Poverty Rates

17.6%

10.6%

Immigrants and Their Children   U.S. Natives and Their Children

■ Poverty Rate

Immigrants and their minor children now account for almost one in four persons living in poverty.

positive attitudes toward education, but by adolescence they can become *disillusioned*, and their attitudes toward teachers and scholastic achievement can become negative and *pessimistic*.

Poverty rates are also higher in immigrant families. This means they may lack access to health care and

Census data indicate that among children in immigrant families, 26% live in linguistically isolated households where no one age 14 or older has a strong command of the English language.

other resources. These families start out being healthier than U.S.-born families, but after they come to this country, poor diet and health care can lower their health levels.

Children can often bounce back and overcome one of these challenges—but when they face several of these challenges at once, their development may be affected.

Hope for the Future

Throughout its history, America has served as the destination point for a steady flow of immigrants. Immi-

Top Ten Foreign Countries - Foreign Born Population Among U.S. Immigrants					
Country	#/year	2000	2004	2010	2010, %
Canada	24,200	678,000	774,800	920,000	2.30%
China	50,900	1,391,000	1,594,600	1,900,000	4.70%
Cuba	14,800	952,000	1,011,200	1,100,000	2.70%
Dominican Republic	24,900	692,000	791,600	941,000	2.30%
El Salvador	33,500	765,000	899,000	1,100,000	2.70%
India	59,300	1,007,000	1,244,200	1,610,000	4.00%
Korea	17,900	701,000	772,600	880,000	2.20%
Mexico	175,900	7,841,000	8,544,600	9,600,000	23.70%
Philippines	47,800	1,222,000	1,413,200	1,700,000	4.20%
Vietnam	33,700	863,000	997,800	1,200,000	3.00%
Total Pop. Top 10	498,900	16,112,000	18,747,600	21,741,000	53.70%
Total Foreign Born	940,000	31,100,000	34,860,000	40,500,000	100%

This table, based on data from the 2000 and 2004 U.S. census, shows the foreign-born population broken down by the most common countries of origin. The last column shows the projected increase in each population by 2010.

grants today come from all around the world. These families bring with them the richness of their separate cultures.

Immigrant families are generally eager and hopeful about the many opportunities this country offers them and their children—but they also fear the possible dangers of their children becoming *too* American, separated from the culture of their country of origin, and more likely to become involved in risky behaviors such as substance abuse or violence. Like all families, they struggle to use their strengths to overcome their challenges.

Immigrants represent about 11% of the U.S. population, but they account for 20% of the low-wage labor force. They are more likely than U.S.-born workers to have only part-time and/or partial-year work, and while 72% of U.S.-born workers have employer-provided health insurance, only 55% of immigrant workers have health insurance provided by their employers.

HEADLINES

(From "In School for the First Time, Teenage Immigrants Struggle" by Jennifer Medina, *New York Times*, January 24, 2009.)

Fanta Konneh is the first girl in her family to go to school. Not the first to go to college, or to graduate from high school. Fanta, 18, who grew up in Guinea after her family fled Liberia, became the first to walk into a classroom of any kind last year.

"Just the boys go to school, so I always knew I was left out," said Fanta, a student at Ellis Preparatory Academy in the South Bronx. "But here, I am trying. I can say many things I did not know before. I can learn things more."

New York City classrooms have long been filled with children from all over the world, and the education challenges they bring with them. But hidden among the nearly 150,000 students across the city still struggling to learn English are an estimated 15,100 who, like Fanta, have had little or no formal schooling and are often illiterate in their native languages.

More than half of these arrive as older teenagers and land in the city's high schools, where they must learn how to learn even as their peers prepare for state subject exams required for a diploma.

"They don't always have a notion of what it means to be a student," said Stephanie Grasso, an English teacher at Ellis Prep, which opened this fall and is New York's first school devoted to this hard-to-educate population. "Certain ideas are completely foreign to them. They have to learn how to ask questions and understand things for themselves."

The largest share of these students come from rural areas of the Dominican Republic, where they did not attend school because it was too far away or because they were working to support their families. Others fled religious persecution in Tibet, civil wars in West Africa or extreme poverty in Central America, often missing years of class while in refugee camps.

According to the official poverty measure, 21% of children with immigrant parents live in poverty, compared with 14% of those with U.S.-born parents.

Children in immigrant families are more than twice as likely as those in U.S.-born families to experience two or more risk factors that may affect normal development.

What Do You Think?

How would it feel to go to school for the first time when you were a teenager? What do you think would frighten you? What would you enjoy?

2 Yesterday's Immigrant Families

Lena Corelli remembers picking wild broccoli at the river's edge every spring. Her parents would round up all four of their children, grab wicker baskets, and walk the eight blocks to the river. There they'd look for the sturdy plants that poked their heads above the grasses and other greenery.

"Remember, don't pull them by their roots, so they can come up again next year," Filomena warned her children in Sicilian, the only language she could speak.

So each child would bend low, breaking the sturdy stems and slowly filling the baskets with the tiny heads of wild broccoli.

Filomena and her husband, Roma, had married in their village in the *old country*, then spent their honeymoon in the bowels of a ship destined for America. They both wiped tears from their cheeks when they saw

Ellis Island

At the mouth of New York City's Hudson River, Ellis Island was once the main entry point for immigrants coming to the United States. Between January 1, 1892 and 1954, Ellis Island processed over 12 million immigrants. Today, over 40 percent of America's population can trace their ancestry through Ellis Island.

The discrimination and racism faced by modern immigrants is not a new phenomenon. This 1888 cartoon depicts concern that immigrants will steal work from United States citizens.

the Statue of Liberty in the distance. They disembarked and made their way into the Ellis Island immigration station.

There they stood in line with other immigrants from Ireland, China, Russia, Greece, and other parts of Europe and Asia, each wearing the garb of his or her native land. One by one, they came before the inspectors with the power to let them into America, pull them into temporary *quarantine*, or ship them back across the ocean. Each person tried to show no fear as the inspectors pulled back their eyelids and thumped their chests, looking and listening for signs of illness or disability that might make them unfit for America's welcome. Those who failed the tests were marked with chalk on their jackets or dresses and promptly separated from the rest.

Filomena stifled the cough she had picked up somewhere in the mid-Atlantic, and the inspector heard no suspicious rumbles in her lungs. So she was free to continue her journey. Roma prided himself on the strength he had gained working in the fields of his homeland. He, too, passed the inspectors' tests and was permitted entry.

They climbed onto the steam-powered train, dragging the trunks that contained all their possessions. Roma was anxious to reunite with his cousin, Guiseppe, whom he hadn't seen for years. Guiseppe had written that his family could share half a bedroom with them while they settled into their new life.

Immigrants are and have always been an essential element in keeping the American economy strong. Today, from fast-food businesses to high-tech industry, they fill a need in the labor force.

Guiseppe introduced them to the foreman in his department at a shoe factory, and within a day both Roma and Filomena had jobs. The work was nothing like they had ever done before, but soon they found a rhythm and were able to keep up with their co-workers who, like Roma and Filomena, were paid by the piece.

In six months they were able to rent their own small place—and in two years their babies began arriving in rapid succession. By that time, Filomena worked from home as a seamstress, the skill she had learned in Sicily, and Roma had moved into another part of the shoe factory. He came home smelling of chemicals—as a little girl, Lena could even smell them on his breath when she hugged him—but he was proud to be able to make a living in this great new country.

With a growing family and a job that paid only a few dollars a week, Roma couldn't plan on being a rich man. But he and Filomena saved every cent they could, and by the time their fourth child was born, they had put a down payment on a three-bedroom house in a working-class neighborhood.

There Lena and her siblings grew up among other immigrant children from Italy and Poland. Language was a barrier that kept the adult neighbors apart, but their children played endless hours together, all in English. At home, Lena's family spoke only Sicilian. Sometimes she would blurt out words in one language when it was

> There were an estimated 34.2 million immigrants in the United States in 2004, according to the U.S. Census Bureau. Of these, 18.3 million came from Latin America, 8.7 million from Asia and 4.7 million from Europe.

time to use the other, an easy mistake, since she was equally fluent in both.

No matter what their nationality, all the families struggled to keep food on the table while adding nickels from every paycheck into their savings accounts. Her father remembered what he had learned in the fields of his village and staked out most of the family's backyard

For immigrants entering New York Harbor on boats bound for Ellis Island, the first glimpses of the Statue of Liberty represented the completion of their difficult journey, and the promise of a new and better life in the United States.

New arrivals to the United States tended to settle in the same communities as other people from their countries. This trend created pockets of other cultures, like Little Italy in New York City (shown here circa 1900).

for a garden. Some in the neighborhood made room for only five or ten tomato plants, but every spring Roma put into the ground hundreds of young tomato, pepper, eggplant, squash, cauliflower and other vegetable plants. The children would harvest lettuce and kale early in the season for the family's daily salads. Then, when the heat of summer brought out other crops, they'd pick string beans and zucchini and onions—and of course tomatoes—for Mama to cook into delicious meals.

Sunday was the day the family ate meat. Other days they feasted on pasta and sauce, soup rich with round beans, and dinners of eggs—from the family's own chickens —and fried potatoes.

When the calendar turned to October, the last of the crops were harvested. Mama canned beets and corn; Papa buried the heartier vegetables in a three-foot deep hole between insulating layers of hay, to be extracted when the snows melted next spring. The children carted potatoes, onion, garlic and root vegetables into the basement where they would be handy all winter.

Mama made the girls' clothes but had to buy them for her son. Like the clothes, shoes were worn until they no longer fit, then passed on to another child. Life was good, Lena says now. They never knew how poor they really were, because all their friends lived the same way.

Lena never felt different from any of her classmates, she says now. Longtime American or first-generation of immigrant parents, there was no difference between them during the day.

By night, though, things were different. Then the immigrants' homes might as well have been in Sicily, with strict rules dictating when to come home, how to line up for evening prayers, and eventually, where to go on dates—and with whom. Her mother had been seventeen when she married, but Lena and her sisters weren't allowed to go on even one date until they had graduated from high school. And no son or daughter was allowed to cast an eye outside the circle of Italian families. "This may be America," Lena's parents told her, "but you must marry an Italian boy."

Fortunately the boy she loved was Italian. They married, and together they raised their own family in their "Little Italy" neighborhood, just down the street from her parents. Now she has great-grandchildren to whom she can tell the stories of her childhood. And this new generation—both the girls AND the boys—are learning the same wonderful recipes Lena learned from her mother.

What Do You Think?

What was the same for Lena's family in the United States as it had been in Italy? What was different? How did Lena's family keep the traditions of their homeland alive in America? Do you envy their close-knit community? Why or why not?

HEADLINES

(From "The Founding Immigrants" by Kenneth C. Davis, *New York Times*, July 3, 2007.)

A prominent American once said, about immigrants, "Few of their children in the country learn English. . . . Unless the stream of their importation could be turned they will soon so outnumber us that all the advantages we have will not be able to preserve our language, and even our government will become *precarious*."

This sentiment did not emerge from the *rancorous* debate over the immigration bill defeated last week in the Senate. . . . Guess again.

Voicing this grievance was Benjamin Franklin. And the language so vexing to him was the German spoken by new arrivals to Pennsylvania in the 1750s, a wave of immigrants whom Franklin viewed as the "most stupid of their nation."

About the same time, a Lutheran minister named Henry Muhlenberg, himself a recent arrival from Germany, worried that "the whole country is being flooded with ordinary, extraordinary and unprecedented wickedness and crimes. . . . Oh, what a fearful thing it is to have so many thousands of unruly and brazen sinners come into this free air and unfenced country."

. . . Once independent, the new nation began to carve its views on immigrants into law. In considering New York's Constitution, for instance, John Jay—later to become the first chief justice of the Supreme Court—suggested erecting "a wall of brass around the country for the exclusion of Catholics."

By 1790, with the United States Constitution firmly in place, the first federal citizenship law restricted naturalization to "free white persons" who had been in the country for two years. That requirement was later pushed back to five years and, in 1798, to 14 years.

. . . [T]his picture of American intolerance clashes sharply with tidy schoolbook images of the great melting pot. Why has the land of "all men are created equal" forged countless ghettoes and intricate networks of social exclusion? Why the signs reading "No Irish Need Apply"? And why has each new generation of immigrants had to face down a rich glossary of now unmentionable epithets? Disdain for what is foreign is, sad to say, as American as apple pie, slavery and lynching.

That fence along the Mexican border now being contemplated by Congress is just the latest vestige of a venerable tradition, at least as old as John Jay's "wall of brass." "Don't fence me in" might be America's unofficial anthem of unfettered freedom, but too often the subtext is, "Fence everyone else out."

What Do You Think?

Why have Americans always worried about immigrants? How do you think these fears affect the lives of immigrant families? In what ways do you think immigrant families are the same today as they were in earlier times? In what ways do you think they will be different?

3 First-Generation Generation Gaps

Terms to Understand

condescension: acting toward a person or group as though they are inferior to oneself.

deterioration: the process of becoming worse, diminishing in quality, character, or value.

heritage: something that comes to a person by birth.

legacy: something handed down from an ancestor or predecessor.

navigating: finding one's way.

liaisons: contacts or connections used to help with communication between people or groups.

assimilate: adapt, or conform to, the customs, styles, values, etc. of a culture.

truancy: the act of being absent without permission.

collective: combined; forming a whole.

menial: lowly, possibly degrading, work.

Valentina tugged at the bow in her hair. Why did she always have to look as though she had never left Pinsk, she grumbled to herself. Her family had been in America three years now, and Ma showed no signs of noticing that styles in their rural corner of White Russia and those here in Buffalo were very different.

Here girls wore pants everywhere, even to church. But telling that to Ma was impossible. The idea of wearing anything but a dress to their Sunday and Wednesday services was unheard of in Ma's mind. Ma wouldn't even let her wear pants to school or own blouses with short sleeves that showed her arms.

Cut her hair into one of those cute styles American girls wore? Not a chance. "A woman's hair is her glory," her mother

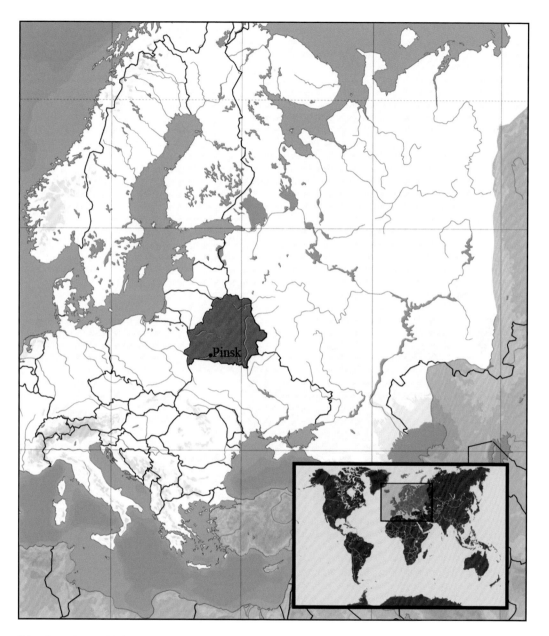

Pinsk, where Valentina and her family are from originally, is a city in the southeastern corner of Belarus.

said, quoting scripture. Valentina loathed her long curls, which blew up like a shaggy balloon on humid days, and she hated still more the ribbons and bows her mother insisted she wear to control her voluminous tresses.

American girls wore gold in their earlobes and chains around their necks—but Valentina couldn't even imagine how Ma would react if she ever wore so much as a simple bracelet.

Almost all teenagers rebel against their parents at some point—it is part of the process of growing up and becoming independent. Like Valentina, children of immigrants may rebel by denying their cultural heritage.

And makeup, forget that! American girls had pinked cheeks and lips, darkened lashes and pastel eyelids, but their look was not for her, said Ma. Never for her.

She was forever in dresses, forever plain, forever labeled an immigrant. She would never do that to her daughter, when she was a mother, she promised herself.

Four years later, when Valentina was twenty, she gave birth to that daughter. No Russian name for her, Valentina told her husband. They named her Brandi, to Ma's great horror.

"Alcohol? You give your child the name of alcohol?" Ma asked, her voice almost a shriek.

But Valentina was determined: the sweet little baby with blond curls and rosebud lips needed an American name—and Valentina thought Brandi was a pretty name.

"You will speak English, only English," Valentina whispered to the baby snuggled in her arms. "You will be an American girl."

Brandi grew into a toddler who explored every corner of the apartment. Ma—now Grandma—watched her and shook her head. "She should have been a boy."

Valentina instantly pointed out that American girls don't have to be silent and always in the background. Their futures were as limitless as a boy's, and their curiosity was to be encouraged, not scowled upon.

Brandi started kindergarten in jeans, a sweatshirt, and a pair of tiny pink sneakers. Her short hair was a halo of golden curls around her head, and pink pearls gleamed in her earlobes.

She loved her grandmother, but she could understand only a few of the words she spoke. When she saw her mother treat her grandmother with scorn, she adopted the same attitude of **condescension** herself.

"No, Grandma, I don't want milk. I like Coke," she said when Grandma gave her buttered raisin bread as a treat.

Valentina experimented with recipes from all over the globe, but she never made borsht or halupki or any of the foods she had known as a girl.

By the time she was twelve, all Brandi's friends had cell phones and electronic toys and music devices. Valentina, eager for Brandi to be a fully American girl, racked up bill after bill on their credit cards.

Makeup? Only a little bit until you're older, she told Brandi.

"Oh, Mother, you're not in Russia anymore, you know," Brandi said disdainfully, using the same tone her mother used with Grandma. She left the house with black slashes around her eyes.

"Brandi—" her mother called. But Brandi was out the door, pretending she hadn't heard.

By then Valentina was in college, learning about child psychology. One textbook gave a case study describing the **deterioration** of an immigrant Southeast Asian family who had come to America when their homeland had become too dangerous. The parents had great difficulty learning English, which used an alphabet and sounds unlike those in any of the dialects they had known in Laos. So their children became their connection to teachers, doctors, and all other Americans—putting the child in a superior position over the parents. Respect quickly disappeared in this upside-down situation. When their son was attracted to a gang, they were unable to influence him.

The ages-old traditions of respect for elders stopped abruptly in such families, and the children separated themselves from the richness of their cultural *heritage*.

Valentina had done much the same thing,

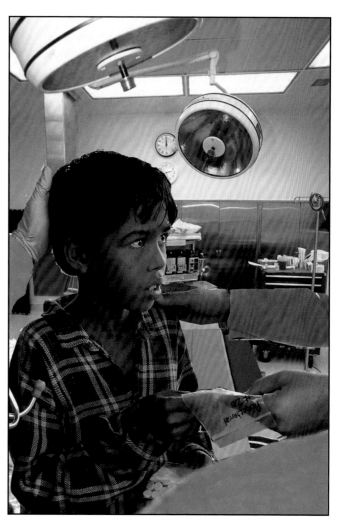

Language is a barrier when immigrants first arrive in the United States—simply communicating with people becomes a challenge. The children, who learn English more quickly, often become translators for their parents.

she realized now. And she was encouraging it in Brandi.

Slowly she introduced into her household the world she had known when she was young. She slid a brightly embroidered cloth, made by her mother years before, onto the center of the dining room table. For Easter she asked her mother to show both Brandi and herself how to make the exquisite eggs of their homeland. She taught Brandi to count in White Russian. Together they cooked

Cooking and eating traditional food is an important part of celebrating a cultural heritage. Halupki, shown here, are cabbage rolls stuffed with ground beef, chopped onions, and rice or barley.

chicken soup with chopped cabbage, just as she remembered her mother making it when she was a girl. And she insisted that Brandi treat her with the same respect that she was now careful to show to her own mother.

Brandi is an American girl. But like every American girl, she has a heritage uniquely her own. To ignore it—or to throw it away—was cheating her out of her ties to her past. It was denying her the richness of her cultural *legacy*.

Brandi wants both a career and to be a mother. She wants to learn to speak Spanish, to cook udon noodles with seaweed and to see a koala bear in person. She wants to be not only American but a citizen of the world.

And now she also has a firm footing in her own heritage, one of the best gifts her mother could ever give her.

What Do You Think?

Did Valentina make a mistake when she tried to be so American that she abandoned all her mother's traditions? Why or why not? Do you agree that it's important for immigrant families to keep the traditions of their homelands? Why or why not? If you were Brandi, how would you feel about the changes Valentina made in their family?

HEADLINES

(From "Conference Eyes Hurdles of Immigrant Teenagers," by Monica Rhor, *Boston Globe*, January 5, 2004.)

In his native Colombia, Felipe's worries centered on school and social life. The biggest challenge he faced was *navigating* the passage between adolescence and adulthood. His mother, a vice president in a flower-exporting company, made a comfortable living and took care of the major decisions in their household.

Then, three years ago, Felipe became seriously ill, and his mother decided to bring the 14-year-old to the United States for treatment. Once here, she decided that the family would not be going back.

Just like that, *en un dos por tres*—like 1-2-3—Felipe became an immigrant, making a leap from country to country and from culture to culture.

For Felipe, now 17, as for other young newcomers, the immigration process was made even more difficult because it was a step forced upon him at a time already fraught with the changes and uncertainties of growing up.

"Here, everything changed completely," said Felipe, speaking in Spanish, who asked that his last name not be used because he is in this country illegally. "Here, I have to help run the house, study, and work. It's very difficult dealing with everything at once."

From Vietnamese teenagers in Dorchester to young Latin American newcomers in East Boston, immigrant youths face . . . myriad . . . hurdles that adult immigrants do not.

No matter where their families come from, the young newcomers often find themselves straddling the lines between cultures: balancing traditions and values maintained by their parents at home, while trying to mesh with their American counterparts at school and on the streets.

Many young immigrants must also serve as their parents' interpreters and *liaisons* to the English–speaking world, a role that places added pressure on teenagers still adjusting to life in an unfamiliar terrain. . . .

Unlike adult immigrants, whose lives in this country often exist within the boundaries of work and home, young newcomers are often thrust unprepared into a society where the language, customs, and laws are different from those of their homelands. As they scramble to adapt to the new, they often find themselves cut off from their traditions, and at odds with their parents.

"You're trying to live in both cultures. You're trying to be American, yet retain your own heritage, and

it's hard to do both," said Samantha Khamvongsa, . . . who experienced a similar tug of war when she came to this country from Laos as a refugee when she was a child. "As a student, you're forced to *assimilate*, because you're meeting other people from other cultures who did not grow up the way you did."

The lessons learned at school and on the streets are often at odds with those passed on at home, said Khamvongsa.

For example, Khamvongsa's father stressed a traditional role for women, saying they should stay at home and serve as homemakers. At school, however, she learned that women can do anything.

"A lot of our youth are very frustrated because they can't communicate with their parents," said Tri Phuong, 24, who works with high-risk Vietnamese teenagers at Tieng Xanh Voice in Dorchester. "They feel like they have to represent their families in terms of being American, and serving as the translators for the parents in official situations. Yet, they can't communicate the reality of their lives to their parents."

For many Vietnamese youth in the Fields Corner neighborhood in Dorchester, that reality includes gangs, *truancy*, interracial squabbles, and often violence, said Phuong, a Harvard graduate who came to this country from Vietnam when he was 7.

Vietnamese teenagers are often caught between an American society that emphasizes individuality, encouraging young people to make their own decisions, and a Vietnamese culture that values the *collective* strength of family, where every decision is made by parents.

"They are digging, sifting through options . . . but they have no role models in ways to live a meaningful, successful life," said Phuong. "They see their parents working *menial* jobs where they are not happy. They see their parents sacrificing for them, but no one is telling them what their goals should be."

In the Vietnamese community, as in most newcomer communities, parents often stress education as the steppingstone for their children's success. However, many young newcomers are blocked from going on to college because of their immigration status. . .

"It's a huge problem that we are facing. Many of us did not make the decision to come here, yet we are paying for it," said Felipe, a high school junior who works in a restaurant to help support his family, and belongs to a group of students lobbying for bills that would lift restrictions on immigrants seeking in-state tuition. "What are we going to do? Spend the rest of our lives washing dishes, or working in factories?"

What Do You Think?

How is American culture different from the culture of many other countries? How do these differences make it difficult for immigrant teenagers? In what ways are immigrant teenagers caught between both generations and cultures?

4 Not Welcome Here

When Miguel Cervantes came to the United States, he left his finger behind.

His parents had chosen a dark, cloudy night to make their dash across the border from Mexico into the United States. Once they made it across, Miguel's uncle Antonio would be waiting to pick them up in San Ysidro. The family would live with Tío Toño while Miguel's parents found work.

Miguel knew his parents were desperate to get away from the violence and poverty that filled Tijuana's streets. On that October night two years earlier, he had been excited to be going to *El Otro Lado*—the Other Side, the term many Mexicans use for the United States—but he was also scared. What if the border patrol officers caught them? Would his parents go to jail?

Miguel's father had climbed to the top of the fence that was meant to keep people like the Cervantes out of the United States. He reached down and gave a hand to Miguel's mother, then helped her straddle the barbed

Terms to Understand

deported: sent out of a country.
undocumented: lacking proper immigration or working papers.

45

wire at the top of the fence. Miguel heard the thud as she landed on the other side. Next his older sister made it over the fence, and then it was Miguel's turn.

"*Está bien, mi hijo,*" his father said. "Now jump. You can do it. I'll go first."

Miguel watched as his father pulled his pant leg free from the barbed wire's grasp and then dropped down on the other side, into the United States. The ground looked very far below him.

And then, as he hesitated there, clinging to the top of the fence, the thing he had feared most happened: he heard the sound of an engine coming toward him, and then a long white, finger of light slid through the darkness, searching for him. With a gasp, he flung himself over the fence, becoming tangled in the wire.

For what seemed like an eternity, he hung like a fly in a spider web, feeling the wire biting his hand and arm. Then his father yanked on his other arm and pulled him free. Pain shot through Miguel's hand, but there was no time for him to think about it. His father tucked him under his arm and ran with him, while something warm and hot spilled from Miguel's hand.

Miguel nearly died that night from loss of blood. His parents did not dare to take him to a hospital, so his mother tied a strip from her skirt tight around his hand to stop the bleeding from his severed finger. That was the last thing Miguel remembers clearly from the night he came to America.

The border between Tijuana and the United States is busy—in 2005 about 50 million people entered the United States at the San Ysidro, California, port of entry.

Now, two years later, he has become used to his missing finger. It does not keep him from working at his father's and his uncle's sides, picking strawberries and other fruit in the fields of California. In fact, he is the fastest picker in his family.

Foreign-born workers, like these strawberry pickers, form a large share of the hired crop labor force. According to the National Agricultural Workers Survey, from 2001–2002, seventy-five percent of crop laborers were born in Mexico, two percent were from Central American countries, and one percent of the workers were from elsewhere.

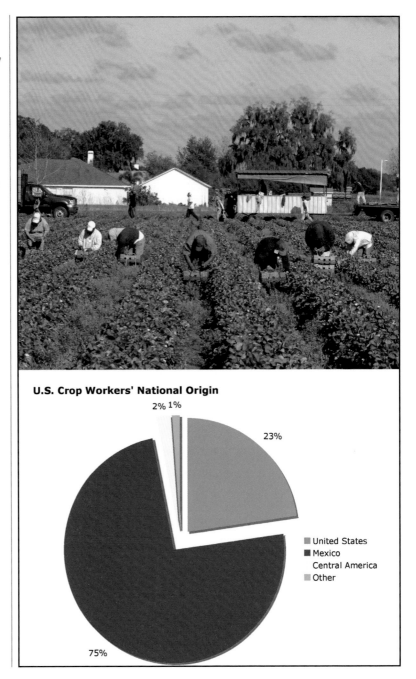

U.S. Crop Workers' National Origin

2% 1%

23%

United States
Mexico
Central America
Other

75%

Unfounded Prejudice

Many white Americans worry about the flood of Hispanic immigrants coming into the United States. They fear that these people will change America and make it a country with weaker morals and less ambition. According to research conducted by political scientists from the University of Berkeley, however, Americans have no reason to worry that Hispanic immigrants are a threat to America's identity. The research showed:

- By the second generation, children of Hispanic immigrants speak English as their first language.
- Hispanic immigrants are as religious as native-born whites.
- Hispanics are even more committed to a strict work ethic than are native-born whites.
- By the second and third generations, the children of Hispanic immigrants show levels of patriotism that equals that of native-born whites.

Miguel is proud that he can earn money for his family. "I do not ever regret that we came here," he says. "Life is better for us all here. We are safer, we eat better, we are happier. My father and I can take better care of my sister and my mother."

Immigrant Hatred

In March of 2006, New Jersey-based neo-Nazi radio host Hal Turner called for the mass murder of Hispanics and the assassination of U.S. senators who support guest worker programs. "I advocate using extreme violence against illegal aliens. Clean your guns. Have plenty of ammunition. Find out where the largest gathering of illegal aliens will be near you. Go to the area well in advance, scope out several places to position yourself and then do what has to be done." Turner directed his listeners to a website that provides detailed instructions on constructing pipe bombs, ammonium nitrate "fertilizer bombs," car bombs, chlorine gas bombs, and other homemade explosive devices.

Meanwhile, in California, the leader of the hate group Save our State, Joe Turner, obtained enough signatures from residents of San Bernardino to get an immigrant-bashing initiative he authored on the upcoming ballot. Turner's "City of San Bernardino Illegal Immigration Relief Act" would prohibit city funding of day laborer centers, allow police to seize the vehicles of anyone hiring an *undocumented* day laborer, and make it a crime for landlords to rent to illegal immigrants. The Supreme Court struck down the act saying Turner had not gathered enough signatures to qualify the measure. Turner vowed to bring a new, harsher measure to the ballot.

A National Guard soldier, armed with an M16 weapon, stands watch, scanning the city through his binoculars, on the United States border with Mexico at Nogales, Arizona. Since September 11, 2001, there has been increased security along the U.S.-Mexico border.

Illegal aliens contribute about as much to the public coffers in taxes as they receive in benefits. New data suggests the undocumented pay about 46% as much in taxes as do natives, but use about 45% as much in services. A poll of the most respected economists found a consensus that both legal and illegal immigrants are beneficial economically.

Hate Crimes and Immigrants

Another growing immigrant group experiencing an upsurge in hate crime, largely as a result of Middle East crises and the September 11, 2001 terrorist attacks, are people of Arab descent. Often they are blamed for incidents to which they have no connection. The hate crimes following the 9/11 terrorist attacks, which included murder and beatings, were directed at Arabs solely because they shared or were perceived as sharing the national background of the hijackers responsible for attacking the World Trade Center and the Pentagon.

According to Hispanic traditions, it is men's job to protect the women in his family, and Miguel takes this responsibility seriously. "My family is the most important thing in my life," he says. "It makes me angry when I see my father and my uncle being looked down on. When men say rude things to my sister, I want to hit them—but I know I must be careful. If I get in a fight and the police are called, I will be *deported*. I do not want to be separated from my family. So we are always careful."

Miguel says he knows that people like him and his family are not welcome in the United States, even though there are plenty of jobs for them to do. "Some-day I would like to be an American. I would like to go to school, and learn how to be something besides a fruit picker one day. But I know that will probably never happen."

Miguel looks down at the stump of his missing finger. "I left a piece of myself behind in Mexico. So I am not sure if I will ever really belong here."

What Do You Think?

Compare Miguel's experiences to those of Lina's in chapter 2. In what ways do you think they are similar? In what ways are they very different? What explains these differences? Do you think Miguel and his family have a right to be in the United States? Why or why not?

According to hate crime statistics published annually by the FBI, anti-Latino hate crimes rose by almost 35% between 2003 and 2006.

HEADLINES

(From "Dozens of U.S. Citizens Locked Up as Illegal Immigrants in Past 8 Years," AP News, April 12, 2009.)

Pedro Guzman has been an American citizen all his life. Yet in 2007, the 31-year-old Los Angeles native—in jail for a misdemeanor, mentally ill and never able to read or write—signed a waiver agreeing to leave

Many people are against the increases in immigration detentions and deportations. These people, in Chicago, IL, are marching in support of immigrant workers and in protest of deportations.

the country without a hearing and was deported to Mexico as an illegal immigrant.

For almost three months, Guzman slept in the streets, bathed in filthy rivers and ate out of trash cans while his mother scoured the city of Tijuana, its hospitals and morgues, clutching his photo in her hand. He was finally found trying to cross the border at Calexico, 100 miles away.

These days, back home in California, "He just changes from one second to another. His brain jumps back

to when he was missing," said his brother, Michael Guzman. "We just talk to him and reassure him that everything is fine and nobody is going to hurt him."

In a drive to crack down on illegal immigrants, the United States has locked up or thrown out dozens, probably many more, of its own citizens over the past eight years. A months-long Associated Press investigation has documented 55 such cases, on the basis of interviews, lawsuits and documents obtained under the Freedom of Information Act. These citizens are detained for anything from a day to five years. Immigration lawyers say there are actually hundreds of such cases.

It is illegal to deport U.S. citizens or detain them for immigration violations. Yet citizens still end up in detention because the system is overwhelmed, acknowledged Victor Cerda, who left Immigration and Customs Enforcement in 2005 after overseeing the system. The number of detentions overall is expected to rise by about 17 percent this year to more than 400,000, putting a severe strain on the enforcement network and legal system.

The result is the detention of citizens with the fewest resources: the mentally ill, minorities, the poor, children and those with outstanding criminal warrants, ranging from unpaid traffic tickets to failure to show

up for probation hearings. Most at risk are Hispanics, who made up the majority of the cases the AP found. . . .

What is clear is that immigration detentions—including those of citizens—have soared in recent years. One reason is a heightened concern for security that arose out of the Sept. 11, 2001, terrorist attacks. Another is a political climate that encouraged a tough stance on illegal immigration, especially after Congress failed to pass immigration reform legislation almost three years ago. . . .

On the day he arrived in Mexico, Guzman called a relative to say he didn't know where he was, and asked a passer-by. The answer: Tijuana. Then the phone cut off.

Guzman was finally returned to California legally in August 2007.

Now he can no longer stand the sun because it reminds him of Mexico. His family will not let him talk about the ordeal because it upsets him. He has frequent counseling sessions, but he is shaky, stutters and seems to hear voices, according to his brother.

"He is our brother, somebody's son, that they deported," said Michael Guzman. . . . The family has sued Los Angeles County and the federal government. . . . In the meantime, Guzman's mother, Maria Carbajal, often works the graveyard shift at a Jack in the Box because she is afraid to leave him alone during the day.

. . . For Ricardo Martinez, born in McAllen, Texas, it was not being able to get back into his own country.

Even though he was a U.S. citizen, Martinez lived in Mexico between the ages of 5 and 17.

Like many border residents with family on the other side, he made frequent trips to Mexico. . . . In January 2006, he went back to Mexico to be with his dying grandmother. When he tried to cross back at Laredo, Texas, in March, he carried his birth certificates, his birth registration card, his passport and state ID cards from Nebraska, California and Texas, where he had worked.

. . . Agents . . . claimed his U.S. passport was fake, he said.

Martinez was taken to an inspection room, forced to remove his shoes, searched, handcuffed to a chair and held for two hours while officers questioned his documents, he said. He was told unless he confessed to fraud, he would be sent to prison for six to eight months, according to a court document filed in Martinez's lawsuit against the government.

"They told me if I didn't say I was from over there, they would put me in jail. I was frightened," Martinez said.

He said he asked to call his mother to help prove his citizenship, but was refused.

Martinez's stepfather, Florentino Mireles, said in a Feb. 27, 2008, affidavit that he called border inspectors to ask why they had taken Martinez's documents. The response, he said: An officer didn't believe Martinez was a U.S. citizen because he didn't speak English.

Afraid of jail, Martinez signed the papers. In an affidavit in his lawsuit, Martinez said he didn't understand that by signing he was admitting to not being born in the U.S.

It took his parents two years to find an affordable attorney. Finally, at a meeting in Hidalgo, attorney Lisa Brodyaga showed border officers a copy of Martinez' birth certificate from his parents that included his footprints and a thumbprint and tax records showing he had worked legally in the U.S. Officials agreed he was a U.S. citizen and allowed him to cross the border. . . .

Brodyaga said the cases of U.S. citizens detained or deported show more than bureaucratic bungling.

"I've been doing this for 30 years and I've seen bureaucratic bungling. This is more than that," she said. "This is an atmosphere of suspicion and hostility, particularly for Mexican-Americans on the border."

What Do You Think?

According to this article, what event caused the increased suspicion many Americans feel toward immigrants? Do you think these suspicions are justified? Why or why not?

What role does family play in both the stories related in this article (Pedro Guzman's and Ricardo Martinez's)?

In your opinion, is it more important to protect Americans from possible terrorists who might come across U.S. borders illegally—or to respect the rights of immigrants? Why?

Find Out More
BOOKS

Biddle, Wendy. *Immigrants' Rights After 9/11*. New York: Chelsea House, 2008.

Blohm, Judith M. and Terri Lapinski. *Kids Like Me: Voices of the Immigrant Experience*. Boston: Intercultural Press, 2006.

Budhos, Marina. *Remix: Conversations with Immigrant Teenagers*. Eugene, Ore.: Resource Publications, 2007.

Foner, Nancy. *Across Generations: Immigrant Families in America*. New York: NYU Press, 2009.

Gallo, Donald R., ed. *First Crossings: Stories About Teen Immigrants*. Cambridge, Mass.: Candlewick Press, 2007.

Garrison, Philip. *Because I Don't Have Wings: Stories of Mexican Immigrant Life*. Tucson, Ariz.: University of Arizona Press, 2006.

Hernandez, Roger E. *Immigration*. Broomall, Pa.: Mason Crest Publishers, 2006.

Langley, Andrew. *How Much Should Immigration Be Restricted?* Portsmouth, N.H.: Heinemann, 2007.

Martinez, Ruben. *Crossing Over: A Mexican Family on the Migrant Trail.* New York: Picador, 2002.

Young, Mitchell, ed. *Immigration*. Chicago: Greenhaven Press, 2007.

ON THE INTERNET

American Civil Liberties Union: Immigrants
www.aclu.org/immigrants/index

Ellis Island
www.ellisisland.org

Justice for Immigrants: A Journey of Hope
www.justiceforimmigrants.org

National Center for Children in Poverty: Immigrant Families
www.nccp.org/topics/immigrantfamilies

National Immigration Forum
www.immigrationforum.org

Bibliography

American Academy of Child & Adolescent Psychiatry. "Facts for Families: Multiracial Children." www.aacap.org/cs/root/facts_for_families/multiracial_children.

Blackmon, J. "Multi-Colored Families: Racially Mixed Households Face Their Own Challenges: Hear How They Are Trying to Meet Them." *Time*. May 3, 1999, p. 80A(1).

Cohn, D, and D. Fears. "Multiracial Growth Seen in Census: Numbers Show Diversity, Complexity of U.S. Count." *The Washington Post*. March 13, 2001 p. A01.

"Color My World: The Promise and Perils of Life in the New Multiracial Mainstream." *Newsweek*. May 8, 2000, p. 70.

"Race: The Power of an Illusion." PBS. www.pbs.org/race/000_General/000_00-Home.htm

Index

About the Author and the Consultant

AUTHOR

Julianna Fields is the pseudonym of a Gannett human interest columnist whose byline has also appeared in *Writer's Digest*, *American History*, *American Woodworker* and hundreds of other publications, as well as educational workbooks and a guidebook about Steamtown, a National Park Service site in Scranton, Pennsylvania. She's also a writing coach and editor.

CONSULTANT

Gallup has studied human nature and behavior for more than seventy years. Gallup's reputation for delivering relevant, timely, and visionary research on what people around the world think and feel is the cornerstone of the organization. Gallup employs many of the world's leading scientists in management, economics, psychology, and sociology, and its consultants assist leaders in identifying and monitoring behavioral economic indicators worldwide. Gallup consultants help organizations boost organic growth by increasing customer engagement and maximizing employee productivity through measurement tools, coursework, and strategic advisory services. Gallup's 2,000 professionals deliver services at client organizations, through the Web, at Gallup University's campuses, and in forty offices around the world.